*New & Selected Poems*

THE UNIVERSITY OF CHICAGO PRESS

*New*

*&*

*Selected*

*Poems*

*by*

*Howard Nemerov*

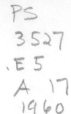
The poems in Part I have not previously been collected; they appeared in the following periodicals: AUDIENCE, THE CARLETON MISCELLANY, THE COLORADO REVIEW, THE AMERICAN SCHOLAR, THE NEW YORKER, POETRY, THE NOBLE SAVAGE, THE NATION, NEW WORLD WRITING, THE PARTISAN REVIEW.

The poems in Part II are selected from THE SALT GARDEN *(1955) and* MIRRORS & WINDOWS *(1958); those in Part III from* THE IMAGE & THE LAW *(1947) and* GUIDE TO THE RUINS *(1950).*

*Library of Congress Catalog Card Number: 60-14236*

THE UNIVERSITY OF CHICAGO PRESS, CHICAGO 60637

THE UNIVERSITY OF CHICAGO PRESS, LTD., LONDON W.C. 1

# Contents

*Part I*

*New Poems*

# Moment

Now, starflake frozen on the windowpane
All of a winter night, the open hearth
Blazing beyond Andromeda, the sea-
Anemone and the downwind seed, O moment
Hastening, halting in a clockwise dust,
The time in all the hospitals is now,
Under the arc-lights where the sentry walks
His lonely wall it never moves from now,
The crying in the cell is also now,
And now is quiet in the tomb as now
Explodes inside the sun, and it is now
In the saddle of space, where argosies of dust
Sail outward blazing, and the mind of God,
The flash across the gap of being, thinks
In the instant absence of forever: now.

# Runes

"... *insaniebam salubriter et moriebar vitaliter.*"

ST. AUGUSTINE

I

This is about the stillness in moving things,
In running water, also in the sleep
Of winter seeds, where time to come has tensed
Itself, enciphering a script so fine
Only the hourglass can magnify it, only
The years unfold its sentence from the root.
I have considered such things often, but
I cannot say I have thought deeply of them:
That is my theme, of thought and the defeat
Of thought before its object, where it turns
As from a mirror, and returns to be
The thought of something and the thought of thought,
A trader doubly burdened, commercing
Out of one stillness and into another.

II

About Ulysses, the learned have reached two
Distinct conclusions. In one, he secretly
Returns to Ithaca, is recognized
By Euryclea, destroys the insolent suitors,
And makes himself known to Penelope,
Describing the bed he built; then, at the last
Dissolve, we see him with Telemachus
Leaving the palace, planning to steal sheep:
The country squire resumes a normal life.
But in the other, out beyond the gates
Of Hercules, gabbling persuasively
About virtue and knowledge, he sails south
To disappear from sight behind the sun;
Drowning near blessed shores he flames in hell.
I do not know which ending is the right one.

4

III

Sunflowers, traders rounding the horn of time
Into deep afternoons, sleepy with gain,
The fall of silence has begun to storm
Around you where you nod your heavy heads
Whose bare poles, raking out of true, will crack,
Driving your wreckage on the world's lee shore.
Your faces no more will follow the sun,
But bow down to the ground with a heavy truth
That dereliction learns, how charity
Is strangled out of selfishness at last;
When, golden misers in the courts of summer,
You are stripped of gain for coining images
And broken on this quarter of the wheel,
It is on savage ground you spill yourselves,
And spend the tarnished silver of your change.


IV

The seed sleeps in the furnaces of death,
A cock's egg slept till hatching by a serpent
Wound in his wintry coil, a spring so tight
In his radical presence that every tense
Is now. Out of this head the terms of kind,
Distributed in syntax, come to judgment,
Are basilisks who write our sentences
Deep at the scripture's pith, in rooted tongues,
How one shall marry while another dies.
Give us our ignorance, the family tree
Grows upside down and shakes its heavy fruit,
Whose buried stones philosophers have sought.
For each stone bears the living word, each word
Will be made flesh, and all flesh fall to seed:
Such stones from the tree; and from the stones, such blood.

V

The fat time of the year is also time
Of the Atonement; birds to the berry bushes,
Men to the harvest; a time to answer for
Both present plenty and emptiness to come.
When the slain legal deer is salted down,
When apples smell like goodness, cold in the cellar,
You hear the ram's horn sounded in the high
Mount of the Lord, and you lift up your eyes
As though by this observance you might hide
The dry husk of an eaten heart which brings
Nothing to offer up, no sacrifice
Acceptable but the canceled-out desires
And satisfactions of another year's
Abscess, whose zero in His winter's mercy
Still hides the undecipherable seed.

VI

White water now in the snowflake's prison,
A mad king in a skullcap thinks these thoughts
In regular hexagons, each one unlike
Each of the others. The atoms of memory,
Like those that Democritus knew, have hooks
At either end, but these? Insane tycoon,
These are the riches of order snowed without end
In this distracted globe, where is no state
To fingerprint the flakes or number these
Moments melting in flight, seeds mirroring
Substance without position or a speed
And course unsubstanced. What may the spring be,
Deep in the atom, among galactic snows,
But the substance of things hoped for, argument
Of things unseen? White water, fall and fall.

*Unstable as water, thou shalt not excel*
—Said to the firstborn, the dignity and strength,
And the defiler of his father's bed.
Fit motto for a dehydrated age
Nervously watering whisky and stock,
Quick-freezing dreams into realities.
Brain-surgeons have produced the proustian syndrome,
But patients dunk their tasteless madeleines
In vain, those papers that the Japanese
Amused themselves by watering until
They flowered and became Combray, flower
No more. The plastic and cosmetic arts
Unbreakably record the last word and
The least word, till sometimes even the Muse,
In her transparent raincoat, resembles a condom.

VIII

To go low, to be as nothing, to die,
To sleep in the dark water threading through
The fields of ice, the soapy, frothing water
That slithers under the culvert below the road,
Water of dirt, water of death, dark water,
And through the tangle of the sleeping roots
Under the coppery cold beech woods, the green
Pinewoods, and past the buried hulls of things
To come, and humbly through the breathing dreams
Of all small creatures sleeping in the earth;
To fall with the weight of things down on the one
Still ebbing stream, to go on to the end
With the convict hunted through the swamp all night.
The dog's corpse in the ditch, to come at last
Into the pit where zero's eye is closed.

IX

In this dehydrated time of digests, pills
And condensations, the most expensive presents
Are thought to come in the smallest packages:
In atoms, for example. There are still
To be found, at carnivals, men who engrave
The Lord's Prayer on a grain of wheat for pennies,
But they are a dying race, unlike the men
Now fortunate, who bottle holy water
In plastic tears, and bury mustard seeds
In lucite lockets, and for safety sell
To be planted on the dashboard of your car
The statues, in durable celluloid,
Of Mary and St. Christopher, who both
With humble power in the world's floodwaters
Carried their heavy Savior and their Lord.

X

White water, white water, feather of a form
Between the stones, is the race run to stay
Or pass away? Your utterance is riddled,
Rainbowed and clear and cold, tasting of stone,
Its brilliance blinds me. But still I have seen,
White water, at the breaking of the ice,
When the high places render up the new
Children of water and their tumbling light
Laughter runs down the hills, and the small fist
Of the seed unclenches in the day's dazzle,
How happiness is helpless before your fall,
White water, and history is no more than
The shadows thrown by clouds on mountainsides,
A distant chill, when all is brought to pass
By rain and birth and rising of the dead.

## XI

A holy man said to me, "Split the stick
And there is Jesus." When I split the stick
To the dark marrow and the splintery grain
I saw nothing that was not wood, nothing
That was not God, and I began to dream
How from the tree that stood between the rivers
Came Aaron's rod that crawled in front of Pharaoh,
And came the rod of Jesse flowering
In all the generations of the Kings,
And came the timbers of the second tree,
The sticks and yardarms of the holy three-
masted vessel whereon the Son of Man
Hung between thieves, and came the crown of thorns,
The lance and ladder, when was shed that blood
Streamed in the grain of Adam's tainted seed.

## XII

Consider how the seed lost by a bird
Will harbor in its branches most remote
Descendants of the bird; while everywhere
And unobserved, the soft green stalks and tubes
Of water are hardening into wood, whose hide,
Gnarled, knotted, flowing, and its hidden grain,
Remember how the water is streaming still.
Now does the seed asleep, as in a dream
Where time is compacted under pressures of
Another order, crack open like stone
From whose division pours a stream, between
The raindrop and the sea, running in one
Direction, down, and gathering in its course
That bitter salt which spices us the food
We sweat for, and the blood and tears we shed.

XIII

There sailed out on the river, Conrad saw,
The dreams of men, the seeds of commonwealths,
The germs of Empire. To the ends of the earth
One many-veined bloodstream swayed the hulls
Of darkness gone, of darkness still to come,
And sent its tendrils steeping through the roots
Of wasted continents. That echoing pulse
Carried the ground swell of all sea-returns
Muttering under history, and its taste,
Saline and cold, was as a mirror of
The taste of human blood. The sailor leaned
To lick the mirror clean, the somber and
Immense mirror that Conrad saw, and saw
The other self, the sacred Cain of blood
Who would seed a commonwealth in the Land of Nod.

XIV

There is a threshold, that meniscus where
The strider walks on drowning waters, or
That tense, curved membrane of the camera's lens
Which darkness holds against the battering light
And the distracted drumming of the world's
Importunate plenty.—Now that threshold,
The water of the eye where the world walks
Delicately, is as a needle threaded
From the reel of a raveling stream, to stitch
Dissolving figures in a watered cloth,
A damask either-sided as the shroud
Of the lord of Ithaca, labored at in light,
Destroyed in darkness, while the spidery oars
Carry his keel across deep mysteries
To harbor in unfathomable mercies.

XV

To watch water, to watch running water
Is to know a secret, seeing the twisted rope
Of runnels on the hillside, the small freshets
Leaping and limping down the tilted field
In April's light, the green, grave and opaque
Swirl in the millpond where the current slides
To be combed and carded silver at the fall;
It is a secret. Or it is not to know
The secret, but to have it in your keeping,
A locked box, Bluebeard's room, the deathless thing
Which it is death to open. Knowing the secret,
Keeping the secret—herringbones of light
Ebbing on beaches, the huge artillery
Of tides—it is not knowing, it is not keeping,
But being the secret hidden from yourself.

# On Certain Wits

*who amused themselves over the simplicity of
Barnett Newman's paintings shown at Bennington
College in May of 1958*

When Moses in Horeb struck the rock,
And water came forth out of the rock,
Some of the people were annoyed with Moses
And said he should have used a fancier stick.

And when Elijah on Mount Carmel brought the rain,
Where the prophets of Baal could not bring rain,
Some of the people said that the rituals of the prophets of Baal
Were aesthetically significant, while Elijah's were very plain.

# To H. M.

*On Reading His Poems*

As when the gannet goes deep down
And splashes like a stone,
The splash may be windblown
Until a rainbow in the spray
Scatters and falls away
Whether or no the gannet gets his fish:—
So with the poet and the secret wish.

## Maestria

Is where you find it,
And you need not agree with its views
About money or the meaning of numbers,
About the immaculate conception or the divine
Ancestry of Augustus. After a few years,
The smoke having blown off those battlefields
And the dead having buried their dead,
Only the scholar will revisit that silence
To inspect the rusting, controversial wheels
Of the abandoned machinery.
                             There remains
A singular lucidity and sweetness, a way
Of relating the light and the shade,
The light spilling from fountains, the shade
Shaken among the leaves.
                      Doubtless
It would be better to be always right, refraining
From those millennial expectations, but strangely,
Rising sometimes from hatred and wrong,
The song sings itself out to the end,
And like a running stream which purifies itself
It leaves behind the mortality of its maker,
Who has the skill of his art, and a trembling hand.

# Going Away

Now as the year turns toward its darkness
the car is packed, and time come to start
driving west. We have lived here
for many years and been more or less content;
now we are going away. That is how
things happen, and how into new places,
among other people, we shall carry
our lives with their peculiar memories
both happy and unhappy but either way
touched with the strange tonality
of what is gone but inalienable, the clear
and level light of a late afternoon
out on the terrace, looking to the mountains,
drinking with friends. Voices and laughter
lifted in still air, in a light
that seemed to paralyze time.
We have had kindness here, and some
unkindness; now we are going on.
Though we are young enough still
and militant enough to be resolved,
keeping our faces to the front, there is
a moment, after saying all farewells,
when we taste the dry and bitter dust
of everything that we have said and done
for many years, and our mouths are dumb,
and the easy tears will not do. Soon
the north wind will shake the leaves,
the leaves will fall. It may be
never again that we shall see them,
the strangers who stand on the steps,
smiling and waving, before the screen doors
of their suddenly forbidden houses.

# Life Cycle of Common Man

Roughly figured, this man of moderate habits,
This average consumer of the middle class,
Consumed in the course of his average life span
Just under half a million cigarettes,
Four thousand fifths of gin and about
A quarter as much vermouth; he drank
Maybe a hundred thousand cups of coffee,
And counting his parents' share it cost
Something like half a million dollars
To put him through life. How many beasts
Died to provide him with meat, belt and shoes
Cannot be certainly said.
                                    But anyhow,
It is in this way that a man travels through time,
Leaving behind him a lengthening trail
Of empty bottles and bones, of broken shoes,
Frayed collars and worn out or outgrown
Diapers and dinnerjackets, silk ties and slickers.

Given the energy and security thus achieved,
He did . . . ? What? The usual things, of course,
The eating, dreaming, drinking and begetting,
And he worked for the money which was to pay

For the eating, et cetera, which were necessary
If he were to go on working for the money, et cetera,
But chiefly he talked. As the bottles and bones
Accumulated behind him, the words proceeded
Steadily from the front of his face as he
Advanced into the silence and made it verbal.
Who can tally the tale of his words? A lifetime
Would barely suffice for their repetition;
If you merely printed all his commas the result
Would be a very large volume, and the number of times
He said "thank you" or "very little sugar, please,"
Would stagger the imagination. There were also
Witticisms, platitudes, and statements beginning
"It seems to me" or "As I always say."

Consider the courage in all that, and behold the man
Walking into deep silence, with the ectoplastic
Cartoon's balloon of speech proceeding
Steadily out of the front of his face, the words
Borne along on the breath which is his spirit
Telling the numberless tale of his untold Word
Which makes the world his apple, and forces him to eat.

# Boom!

### SEES BOOM IN RELIGION, TOO

*Atlantic City, June 23, 1957* (AP).—*President Eisenhower's pastor said tonight that Americans are living in a period of "unprecedented religious activity" caused partially by paid vacations, the eight-hour day and modern conveniences.*

*"These fruits of material progress," said the Rev. Edward L. R. Elson of the National Presbyterian Church, Washington, "have provided the leisure, the energy, and the means for a level of human and spiritual values never before reached."*

Here at the Vespasian-Carlton, it's just one
religious activity after another; the sky
is constantly being crossed by cruciform
airplanes, in which nobody disbelieves
for a second, and the tide, the tide
of spiritual progress and prosperity
miraculously keeps rising, to a level
never before attained. The churches are full,
the beaches are full, and the filling-stations
are full, God's great ocean is full
of paid vacationers praying an eight-hour day
to the human and spiritual values, the fruits,
the leisure, the energy, and the means, Lord,
the means for the level, the unprecedented level,
and the modern conveniences, which also are full.
Never before, O Lord, have the prayers and praises
from belfry and phonebooth, from ballpark and barbecue
the sacrifices, so endlessly ascended.

It was not thus when Job in Palestine
sat in the dust and cried, cried bitterly;
when Damien kissed the lepers on their wounds
it was not thus; it was not thus
when Francis worked a fourteen-hour day
strictly for the birds; when Dante took
a week's vacation without pay and it rained
part of the time, O Lord, it was not thus.

But now the gears mesh and the tires burn
and the ice chatters in the shaker and the priest
in the pulpit, and Thy Name, O Lord,
is kept before the public, while the fruits
ripen and religion booms and the level rises
and every modern convenience runneth over,
that it may never be with us as it hath been
with Athens and Karnak and Nagasaki,
nor Thy sun for one instant refrain from shining
on the rainbow Buick by the breezeway
or the Chris Craft with the uplift life raft;
that we may continue to be the just folks we are,
plain people with ordinary superliners and
disposable diaperliners, people of the stop'n'shop
'n'pray as you go, of hotel, motel, boatel,
the humble pilgrims of no deposit no return
and please adjust thy clothing, who will give to Thee,
if Thee will keep us going, our annual
Miss Universe, for Thy Name's Sake, Amen.

# Mrs. Mandrill

On the night that Mrs. Mandrill entered Nature,
squirrels and mice and crickets everywhere
were squeaking, while the dark spilled up the sky
and the marble moon rolled out over the hills.

"I had not thought of this," that lady said.
"Involved with crowsfeet, husbands, lawsuits, I
paid it no heed. But now it is plain as day
that subways and wires run among the roots
to stations with outlandish names, if not
no names at all. I can see now," she said,
"how I should have thought of this before I came
out in the noisy night, before I heard
the rumor of betrayal in me, or learned
corruption meant to criticize my heart.
One might have known, though it wasn't said at school,
that there was more to this than met the eye.
Now, I suppose, it is too late." So mooning,
went Mrs. Mandrill over the wild meadows,
through marshes, in the unofficial land
of squirrels and bats and tiny creatures whining
like her refrigerator, where two cold
bottles of milk whitely awaited her
desire, and slowly soured where they stood.

"God?" Mrs. Mandrill said, "I have no God,
and not afraid or ashamed to tell Him so
either, if it should come to that. I am
fatigued, and would find no fault with these arrangements,

did they not cause me pain."
                              But while she said,
her skinny feet troubled the waters, rattled
the leaves, and picked at the nervous vines where crossed
every last telephone in the weird world,
with all the crickety conversations of them
describing how the moon rolled out like a marble,
and how the dark spilled up instead of down.

It was the pain that lady felt, went chirping
through wires and waters of her grasping heart's
exchange, converting stones to vegetables
and blood to stars for sweet speculation's sake.
—"Such unintelligible things." She sighed.
"But they mean me now, and meant me even when
I was a little thing, before my face
broke like a cheese, before my vanity
caught me in netted veins and I went in
for litigation more than lechery.
It hasn't been easy," Mrs. Mandrill cried
to the crickets and other creatures who now silenced
their conversations at her heart, "for though
I knew the lead behind my looking-glass
better than some, I was the more deceived
by the way things looked. But for the love of God
all's one, I see that now, since I shall be
converted even against my will, and my will
converted with me, hearing this creature cry
before her wet heart spills and goes to seed."

# The View from an Attic Window

*for Francis and Barbara*

1.

Among the high-branching, leafless boughs
Above the roof-peaks of the town,
Snowflakes unnumberably come down.

I watched out of the attic window
The laced sway of family trees,
Intricate genealogies

Whose strict, reserved gentility,
Trembling, impossible to bow,
Received the appalling fall of snow.

All during Sunday afternoon,
Not storming, but befittingly,
Out of a still, grey, devout sky,

The snowflakes fell, until all shapes
Went under, and thickening, drunken lines
Cobwebbed the sleep of solemn pines.

Up in the attic, among many things
Inherited and out of style,
I cried, then fell asleep awhile,

Waking at night now, as the snowflakes from darkness to darkness go
Past yellow lights in the street below.

## 2.

I cried because life is hopeless and beautiful.
And like a child I cried myself to sleep
High in the head of the house, feeling the hull
Beneath me pitch and roll among the steep
Mountains and valleys of the many years
    Which brought me to tears.

Down in the cellar, furnace and washing machine,
Pump, fuse-box, water heater, work their hearts
Out at my life, which narrowly runs between
Them and this cemetery of spare parts
For discontinued men, whose hats and canes
    Are my rich remains.

And women, their portraits and wedding gowns
Stacked in the corners, brooding in wooden trunks;
And children's rattles, books about lions and clowns;
And headless, hanging dresses swayed like drunks
Whenever a living footstep shakes the floor;
    I mention no more;

But what I thought today, that made me cry,
Is this, that we live in two kinds of thing:
The powerful trees, thrusting into the sky
Their black patience, are one, and that branching
Relation teaches how we endure and grow;
    The other is the snow,

Falling in a white chaos from the sky,
As many as the sands of all the seas,
As all the men who died or who will die,
As stars in heaven, as leaves of all the trees;
As Abraham was promised of his seed;
    Generations bleed,

Till I, high in the tower of my time
Among familiar ruins, began to cry
For accident, sickness, justice, war and crime,
Because all died, because I had to die.
The snow fell, the trees stood, the promise kept,
    And a child I slept.

## Death and the Maiden

Once I saw a grown man fall from a tree
and die. That's years ago, I was a girl.
My father's house is sold into a home
for the feeble-minded gentlefolk who can't
any longer stand the world, but in those days
there was money to maintain the mile or so
of discipline that kept the hungry grass
parading to the lake, and once a year
bring men to prune the files of giant trees
whose order satisfied and stood for some
euclidean ancestor's dream about the truth:
elms, most of them, already dying of
their yellow blight, and blackened with witches' broom
in the highest branches—but they could die for years,
decades, so tall their silence, and tell you nothing.
Those men came in October every year,
and among the last leaves, the driven leaves,
would set their ladders for assault and swarm
like pirates into the shrouds, thrusting with hook
and long-handled bill against the withered members
of those great corporations, amputating
death away from the center. They were called
tree surgeons, on the ground they were surly-
polite and touched their caps, but in the air
they dared. I would watch one straddle a branch
on a day of rainy wind, his red shirt patched
on the elm's great fan of sky, his pruning-claw
breaking the finger-bones from the high hand
which held him, and I'd dream of voyages.
My father said: "It looks more dangerous
than really it is." But if your hand offend,

I thought, cut off the hand, and if your eye
offend, pluck out the eye. I looked at him
out of my window all one afternoon,
and I think he looked back once, a young man
proud and probably lecherous, while I—
was a maiden at a window. Only he died
that day. "Unlucky boy," my father said,
who then was dying himself without a word
to anyone, the crab's claw tightening
inside the bowel that year to the next
in a dead silence. I do not know if things
that happen can be said to come to pass,
or only happen, but when I remember
my father's house, I imagine sometimes
a dry, ruined spinster at my rainy window
trying to tally on dumb fingers a world's
incredible damage—nothing can stand it!—and
watching the red shirt patched against the sky,
so far and small in the webbed hand of the elm.

# Angel and Stone

In the world are millions and millions of men, and each man,
With a few exceptions, believes himself to be at the center,
A small number of his more or less necessary planets careering
Around him in an orderly manner, some morning stars singing
    together,
More distant galaxies shining like dust in any stray sunbeam
Of his attention. Since this is true not of one man or of two,
But of ever so many, it is hard to imagine what life must be
    like.
But if you drop a stone into a pool, and observe the ripples
Moving in circles successively out to the edges of the pool and
    then
Reflecting back and passing through the ones which continue
    to come
Out of the center over the sunken stone, you observe it is pleas-
    ing.
And if you drop two stones it will still be pleasing, because now
The angular intersections of the two sets form a more compli-
    cated
Pattern, a kind of reticulation regular and of simple origins.
But if you throw a handful of sand into the water, it is con-
    fusion,
Not because the same laws have ceased to obtain, but only
    because
The limits of your vision in time and number forbid you to dis-
    criminate
Such fine, quick, myriad events as the angels and archangels,
    thrones
And dominations, principalities and powers, are delegated to
    witness
And declare the glory of before the Lord of everything that is.

Of these great beings and mirrors of being, little at present is
    known,
And of the manner of their perceiving not much more. We
        imagine them
As benign, as pensively smiling and somewhat coldly smiling,
    but
They may not be as we imagine them. Among them there are
    some who count
The grassblades and the grains of sand by one and one and one
And number the raindrops and memorize the eccentricities of
    snowflakes.
One of the greater ones reckons and records the tides of time,
Distinguishing the dynasties of mountains, races, cities,
As they rise, flower and fall, to whom an age is as a wave,
A nation the spray thrown from its crest; and one, being
    charged
With all the crossing moments, the comings-together and driv-
    ings-apart,
Reads in the chromatin its cryptic scripture as the cell divides;
And one is the watcher over chance events and the guardian of
    disorder
According to the law of the square root of n, so that a certain
    number
Of angels or molecules shall fall in irrelevance and be retro-
    grade.

So do they go, those shining creatures, counting without confusion

And holding in their slow immeasurable gaze all the transactions

Of all the particles, item by atom, while the pyramids stand still

In the desert and the deermouse huddles in his hole and the rain falls

Piercing the skin of the pool with water in water and making a million

And a million designs to be pleasingly latticed and laced and interfused

And mirrored to the Lord of everything that is by one and one and one.

# The Remorse for Time

When I was a boy, I used to go to bed
By daylight, in the summer, and lie awake
Between the cool, white, reconciling sheets,
Hearing the talk of birds, watching the light
Diminish through the shimmering planes of leaf
Outside the window, until sleep came down
When darkness did, eyes closing as the light
Faded out of them, silencing the birds.

Sometimes still, in the sleepless dark hours
Tormented most by the remorse for time,
Only for time, the mind speaks of that boy
(he did no wrong, then why had he to die?)
Falling asleep on the current of the stars
Which even then washed him away past pardon.

# Mousemeal

My son invites me to witness with him
a children's program, a series of cartoons,
on television. Addressing myself to share
his harmless pleasures, I am horrified
by the unbridled violence and hostility
of the imagined world he takes in stride,
where human beings dressed in the skins of mice
are eaten by portcullises and cowcatchers,
digested through the winding corridors
of organs, overshoes, boa constrictors
and locomotive boilers, to be excreted
in waters where shark and squid and abalone
wait to employ their tentacles and jaws.
It seems there is no object in this world
unable to become a gullet with great lonely teeth;
sometimes a set of teeth all by itself
comes clacking over an endless plain
after the moving mouse; and though the mouse
wins in the end, the tail of one cartoon
is spliced into the mouth of the next, where his
rapid and trivial agony repeats itself
in another form. My son has seen these things
a number of times, and knows what to expect;
he does not seem disturbed or anything more
than mildly amused. Maybe these old cartoons
refer to my childhood and not to his
(The ogres in them wear Mussolini's face),
so that when mice are swallowed by skeletons
or empty suits of armor, when a tribe

of savage Negro mice is put through a wringer
and stacked flat in the cellar, he can take
the objective and critical view, while I
am shaken to see the giant picassoid
parents eating and voiding their little mice
time and again. And when the cheery announcer
cries, "Well, kids, that's the end," my son gets up
obediently and runs outside to play.
I hope he will ride over this world as well,
and that his crudest and most terrifying dreams
will not return with such wide publicity.

# The Icehouse in Summer

*see Amos, 3:15*

A door sunk in a hillside, with a bolt
thick as the boy's arm, and behind that door
the walls of ice, melting a blue, faint light,
an air of cedar branches, sawdust, fern:
decaying seasons keeping from decay.

A summer guest, the boy had never seen
(a servant told him of it) how the lake
froze three foot thick, how farmers came with teams,
with axe and saw, to cut great blocks of ice,
translucid, marbled, glittering in the sun,
load them on sleds and drag them up the hill
to be manhandled down the narrow path
and set in courses for the summer's keeping,
the kitchen uses and luxuriousness
of the great houses. And he heard how once
a team and driver drowned in the break of spring:
the man's cry melting from the ice that summer
frightened the sherbet-eaters off the terrace.

Dust of the cedar, lost and evergreen
among the slowly blunting water walls
where the blade edge melted and the steel saw's bite
was rounded out, and the horse and rider drowned
in the red sea's blood, I was the silly child
who dreamed that riderless cry, and saw the guests
run from a ghostly wall, so long before
the winter house fell with the summer house,
and the houses, Egypt, the great houses, had an end.

*Part II*

*Selected Poems 1950–1958*

# *Truth*

Around, above my bed, the pitch-dark fly
Buzzed in the darkness till in my mind's eye
His blue sound made the image of my thought
An image that his resonance had brought
Out of a common midden of the sun—
A garbage pit, and pile where glittering tin
Cans turned the ragged edges of their eyes
In a mean blindness on mine, where the loud flies
Would blur the summer afternoons out back
Beyond the house. Sleepy, insomniac, black
Remainder of a dream, what house? and when?
Listening now, I knew never again
That winged image as in amber kept
Might come, summoned from darkness where it slept
The common sleep of all such sunken things
By the fly's loud buzzing and his dreaming wings.

I listened in an angry wakefulness;
The fly was bitter. Between dream and guess
About a foundered world, about a wrong
The mind refused, I waited long, long,
And then that humming of the garbage heap
I drew beneath the surface of my sleep
Until I saw the helmet of the king
Of Nineveh, pale gold and glittering
On the king's brow, yet sleeping knew that I
But thought the deepening blue thought of the fly.

# The Cuckoo King

My head made wilderness, crowned of weed
And marigold, the world my witching bride
And the half of my kingdom lying in the seed,
I reap the great root of a planted pride.

All earth broken under the harrow's heel,
I through my comely kingdom went a-riding
Out where the bearded grass climbed to rebel
And the tall stalking flower fired from hiding.

The world, O my daughter in the crooked nest,
Bridles with lust, that you by force betray
Me, weed and marigold, to the naked crest
Where castles fall; but I will make this hay
In husbandry beneath the rebel's height,
Though all the hairs of my head stand upright.

# Sleeping Beauty

They told me this story a long time ago,
When I was a child, to make me go to sleep.
I never should have been surprised,
But then, being young, I could not know they meant
My eyes to be the ones that closed
When the time came and the clock struck
And the dream was tolled by the steeple bell.

I listen to the castle sleep, the grooms
In the stables, courtiers on the marble floors,
The scratch of dust descending and the rose
Thickets breaking forth flowers and thorns;
And I ask in sleep, is this my sleep?
Am I the one the wide world cannot find
Nor even the prince in the forest foresee?

This ends only with a kiss, the story said.
Then all the snoring barons will arise
And the dogs begin to bark, the king and queen
Order their coach and four—all on a kiss
The whole world will begin to happen again,
People will yawn, stretch, begin to forget
Whatever they dreamed that was so like a dream.

And shall I also, with the kiss, forget
That I was the one who dreamed them all,
Courtier and king, scullion and cook,
Horse in the stable and fly on the wall?
Forget the petals' whisper when they drift
Down where the untold princes die in blood
Because I dreamed the thicket and the thorn?

# The Quarry

The place is forgotten now; when I was a child
And played here, its ruins were already old
And the cracked granite face already green
To begin again; while now the wild
Overgrowth of briar and birch and pine
Keeps my hollow castle in the hill
Hidden and still.
                              Long silent years
Have split the walls that men with crowbars
And blast had split before; and all repairs
—I know it now—but ravage and ruin again
For the life's sake. The stone and vine-grown crater
I stare on, my dry wound in nature,
Is absence everywhere: what curbs or schools
Or monuments were squared by such rude rules,
Quarried and carried away and dressed in line,
Before the stone could be split by the tree,
And the tree be brought down by the vine?

# *Storm Windows*

People are putting up storm windows now,
Or were, this morning, until the heavy rain
Drove them indoors. So, coming home at noon,
I saw storm windows lying on the ground,
Frame-full of rain; through the water and glass
I saw the crushed grass, how it seemed to stream
Away in lines like seaweed on the tide
Or blades of wheat leaning under the wind.
The ripple and splash of rain on the blurred glass
Seemed that it briefly said, as I walked by,
Something I should have liked to say to you,
Something . . . the dry grass bent under the pane
Brimful of bouncing water . . . something of
A swaying clarity which blindly echoes
This lonely afternoon of memories
And missed desires, while the wintry rain
(Unspeakable, the distance in the mind!)
Runs on the standing windows and away.

# The Pond

At the long meadow's end, where the road runs
High on a bank, making a kind of wall,
The rains of last October slowly built
Us up this pond some hundred yards across
And deep maybe to the height of a man's thigh
At the deepest place. It was surprising how
Slowly the water gained across the land
All autumn, no one noticing, until
We had the pond where none had been before
To any memory—most surprising in
This country where we think of contours as
Fixed on a map and named and permanent,
Where even if a stream runs dry in summer
You have the stream-bed still to go by and
The chartered name—Red Branch, and Henry's Creek,
And Anthony's Race—for reassurance, though
The reason of those names be sunken with
The men who named them so, in the natural past
Before our history began to be
Written in book or map; our history,
Or the settled story that we give the world
Out of the mouths of crones and poachers
Remembering or making up our kinship
In the overgrown swamplands of the mind;
And precious little reassurance, if
You think of it, but enough about that.
Here was, at any rate, surprisingly,
This piece of water covering the ground:
Clear blue, and pale, and crisping up to black
Squalls when the north wind moved across its face;
The question whether it would go or stay

Never came up, and no one gave it a name—
Only the water-birds on their way south
Accepted it, and rested there at night,
Coming at dusk down the meadow on wide wings
And splashing up on beating wings at dawn.

By Christmastime the pond was frozen solid
Under a foot of snow, level and white
Across the meadow so you couldn't say
Except from memory where the water was
And where the land; and maybe no adult
Would have remembered, but the children did
And brought their skates, and someone's father patched
Together a plough from plank and two-by-four
That half-a-dozen kids could lean against
And clear the snow down to the glittering ice.
They skated all the darkening afternoons
Until the sun burnt level on the ice,
And built their fires all along the shore
To warm their hands and feet, and skated nights
Under the full moon or the dark; the ice
Mirrored the moon's light, or the fire's, cold.
There was a tragedy, if that is what
One calls it, the newspapers called it that:
"Pond Claims First Victim" (it still had no name),
As though a monster underneath the ice
Had been in wait to capture the little boy
Skating in darkness all alone, away
From the firelight—the others heard his cry
But he was gone before they found the place—,
Or else as though, a tribe of savages,

We sanctified our sports with sacrifice.
At any rate, the skating didn't stop
Despite the funeral and motherly gloom
And editorials; what happened was
The pond took the boy's name of Christopher,
And this was voted properly in meeting
For a memorial and would be so
On the next map, when the next map was drawn:
*Christopher Pond:* if the pond should still be there.

The winter set its teeth; near Eastertide
Before the pond was free of ice all night;
And by that time the birds were coming back
Leisurely, staying a day or so before
They rose and vanished in the northward sky;
Their lonely cries across the open water
Played on the cold, sweet virginal of spring
A chaste, beginning tune carried along
With a wind out of the east. Killdeer and plover
Came and were gone; grackle, starling and flicker
Settled to stay; and the sparrowhawk would stand
In the height of noon, a stillness on beating wings,
While close over the water swallows would trace
A music nearly visible in air,
Snapping at newborn flies. Slowly the pond
Warmed into life: cocoon and bud and egg,
All winter's seed and shroud, unfolded being
In the pond named for Christopher, who drowned.
By day the birds, and then the frogs at night,
Kept up a music there, part requiem,
Part hunting-song; among the growing reeds

The water boatman worked his oar, the strider
Walked between air and water, dragonfly
Climbed to be born, and dazzled on clear wings.
Then day by day, in the heat of June, the green
World raised itself to natural arrogance,
And the air sang with summer soon to come.

In sullen August, under the massy heat
Of the sun towering in the height, I sat
At the pond's edge, the indeterminate
Soft border of what no longer was a pond
But a swamp, a marsh, with here and there a stretch
Of open water, even that half spread
With lily pads and the rich flesh of lilies.
And elsewhere life was choking on itself
As though, in spite of all the feeding there,
Death could not keep the pace and had to let
Life curb itself: pondweed and pickerel-weed
And bladderwort, eel-grass and delicate
Sundew and milfoil, peopled thick the city
Of themselves; and dragonfly and damselfly
By hundreds darted among the clustering leaves,
Striders by hundreds skated among the stalks
Of pitcher-plant and catkin; breathless the air
Under the intense quiet whining of
All things striving to breathe; the gift of life
Turning its inward heat upon itself.
So, Christopher, I thought, this is the end
Of dedication, and of the small death
We sought to make a name and sacrifice.
The long year has turned away, and the pond
Is drying up, while its remaining life

Grasps at its own throat: the proud lilies wilt,
The milfoil withers, catkins crack and fall,
The dragonfly glitters over it all;
All that your body and your given name
Could do in accidental consecrations
Against nature, returns to nature now,
And so, Christopher, goodbye.

                               But with these thoughts
There came a dragonfly and settled down
On a stem before my eyes, and made me think
How in nature too there is a history,
And that this winged animal of light,
Before it could delight the eye, had been
In a small way a dragon of the deep,
A killer and meat-eater on the floor
Beneath the April surface of the pond;
And that it rose and cast its kind in May
As though putting away costume and mask
In the bitter play, and taking a lighter part.
And thinking so, I saw with a new eye
How nothing given us to keep is lost
Till we are lost, and immortality
Is ours until we have no use for it
And live anonymous in nature's name
Though named in human memory and art.
Not consolation, Christopher, though rain
Fill up the pond again and keep your name
Bright as the glittering water in the spring;
Not consolation, but our acquiescence.
And I made this song for a memorial
Of yourself, boy, and the dragonfly together.

# *Trees*

To be a giant and keep quiet about it,
To stay in one's own place;
To stand for the constant presence of process
And always to seem the same;
To be steady as a rock and always trembling,
Having the hard appearance of death
With the soft, fluent nature of growth,
One's Being deceptively armored,
One's Becoming deceptively vulnerable;
To be so tough, and take the light so well,
Freely providing forbidden knowledge
Of so many things about heaven and earth
For which we should otherwise have no word—
Poems or people are rarely so lovely,
And even when they have great qualities
They tend to tell you rather than exemplify
What they believe themselves to be about,
While from the moving silence of trees,
Whether in storm or calm, in leaf and naked,
Night or day, we draw conclusions of our own,
Sustaining and unnoticed as our breath,
And perilous also—though there has never been
A critical tree—about the nature of things.

# The Murder of William Remington

It is true, that even in the best-run state
Such things will happen; it is true,
What's done is done. The law, whereby we hate
Our hatred, sees no fire in the flue,
But by the smoke, and not for thought alone
It punishes, but for the thing that's done.

And yet there is the horror of the fact,
Though we knew not the man. To die in jail,
To be beaten to death, to know the act
Of personal fury before the eyes can fail
And the man die against the cold last wall
Of the lonely world—and neither is that all:

There is the terror too of each man's thought,
That knows not, but must quietly suspect
His neighbor, friend, or self of being taught
To take an attitude merely correct;
Being frightened of his own cold image in
The glass of government, and his own sin,

Frightened lest senate house and prison wall
Be quarried of one stone, lest righteous and high
Look faintly smiling down and seem to call
A crime the welcome chance of liberty,
And any man an outlaw who aggrieves
The patriotism of a pair of thieves.

## The Sparrow in the Zoo

No bars are set too close, no mesh too fine
To keep me from the eagle and the lion,
Whom keepers feed that I may freely dine.
This goes to show that if you have the wit
To be small, common, cute, and live on shit,
Though the cage fret kings, you may make free with it.

# The Vacuum

The house is so quiet now
The vacuum cleaner sulks in the corner closet,
Its bag limp as a stopped lung, its mouth
Grinning into the floor, maybe at my
Slovenly life, my dog-dead youth.

I've lived this way long enough,
But when my old woman died her soul
Went into that vacuum cleaner, and I can't bear
To see the bag swell like a belly, eating the dust
And the woolen mice, and begin to howl

Because there is old filth everywhere
She used to crawl, in the corner and under the stair.
I know now how life is cheap as dirt,
And still the hungry, angry heart
Hangs on and howls, biting at air.

*Reflexions on the Seizure of the Suez, and on a Proposal to Line the Banks of That Canal with Billboard Advertisements*

From Molepolole and Morogoro,
Dongola, Dungun, Dush,
From Kongor and Gojjam and Juba,
Gagag and Segag and Geba Geba,
The bracelets of brass and the calico hankies
Come back a thousandfold.

*Smoke Pyramids for Appearances' Sake*

From Kanker and Kurnool and Bhor,
Bellary, Trivandrum, Nellore,
From Gooty and Owsa, Hubh and Alur,
Adoni and Chik- and Dod-Ballapur,
The glass beads and obsolete Lee Enfields
Return upon the makers

*Drink Pyramids the World's Premier Aperient*

In Hebron, Jabal, Zebara,
In Jebel Tathlith and Wafi Harid,
Asterabad, Washraf, Miskin, Sham,
In Jask and Ras Nus, Beni Auf, Jauf,
It is the same. Everywhere the givers
Are in the hands of the receivers.

*For That Serious Fear, Take a Pyramid*

So also in Bumpass and Mauch Chunk,
Tallulah, Wabuska, Markle and Lair,
The burden of Tupelo, Tunica, Nampa, Dufur,
Of Grundy and Presho and Stackhouse and Bland.
Though oil cast upon the troubled waters
May be returned as capital gains.

   *Pyramids Are Silent, Speedy, Safe.*
      *—Next Time, Go by Pyramid.*

# The Statues in the Public Gardens

Alone at the end of green *allées*, alone
Where a path turns back upon itself, or else
Where several paths converge, green bronze, grey stone,
The weatherbeaten famous figures wait
Inside their basins, on their pedestals,
Till time, as promised them, wears out of date.

Around them rise the willow, birch, and elm,
Sweet shaken pliancies in the weather now.
The granite hand is steady on the helm,
The sword, the pen, unshaken in the hand,
The bandage and the laurel on the brow:
The last obedience is the last command.

Children and nurses eddying through the day,
Old gentlemen with newspapers and canes,
And licit lovers, public as a play,
Never acknowledge the high regard of fame
Across their heads—the patriot's glare, the pains
Of prose—and scarcely stop to read a name.

Children, to be illustrious is sad.
Do not look up. Those empty eyes are stars,
Their glance the constellation of the mad
Who must be turned to stone. To save your garden,
My playful ones, those pallid voyagers
Stand in the streak of rain, imploring pardon.

At night the other lovers come to play
Endangered games, and robbers lie in wait
To knock old ladies with a rock; but they
Tremble to come upon these stony men
And suffragettes, who shine like final fate
In the electric green of every glen.

For it is then that statues suffer their
Sacrificed lives, and sigh through fruitless trees
After the flesh. Their sighs tremble the air,
They would surrender scepters, swords, and globes,
Feeling the soft flank shudder to the breeze
Under the greatcoats and the noble robes.

In darker glades, the nearly naked stone
Of athlete, goddess chaste as any snows
That stain them winters, tempts maiden and man
From their prosthetic immortality:
Pythagoras' thigh, or Tycho's golden nose,
For a figleaf fallen from the withered tree.

# A Primer of the Daily Round

A peels an apple, while B kneels to God,
C telephones to D, who has a hand
On E's knee, F coughs, G turns up the sod
For H's grave, I do not understand
But J is bringing one clay pigeon down
While K brings down a nightstick on L's head,
And M takes mustard, N drives into town,
O goes to bed with P, and Q drops dead,
R lies to S, but happens to be heard
By T, who tells U not to fire V
For having to give W the word
That X is now deceiving Y with Z,
   Who happens just now to remember A
   Peeling an apple somewhere far away.

# Absent-Minded Professor

This lonely figure of not much fun
Strayed out of folklore fifteen years ago
Forever. Now on an autumn afternoon,
While the leaves drift past the office window,
His bright replacement, present-minded, stays
At the desk correcting papers, nor ever grieves
For the silly scholar of the bad old days,
Who'd burn the papers and correct the leaves.

# Painting a Mountain Stream

Running and standing still at once
is the whole truth. Raveled or combed,
wrinkled or clear, it gets its force
from losing force. Going it stays.

Pulse beats, and planets echo this,
the running down, the standing still,
all thunder of the one thought.
The mind that thinks it is unfounded.

I speak of what is running down.
Of sun, of thunder bearing the rain
I do not speak, of the rising flame
or the slow towering of the elm.

A comb was found in a girl's grave
(ah heartsblood raveled like a rope).
The visible way is always down
but there is no floor to the world.

Study this rhythm, not this thing.
The brush's tip streams from the wrist
of a living man, a dying man.
The running water is the wrist.

In the confluence of the wrist
things and ideas ripple together,
as in the clear lake of the eye,
unfathomably, running remains.

The eye travels on running water,
out to the sky, if you let it go.
However often you call it back
it travels again, out to the sky.

The water that seemed to stand is gone.
The water that seemed to run is here.
Steady the wrist, steady the eye;
paint this rhythm, not this thing.

# Sarabande

*Honoring the Musicians*

Whatever may be going through our heads
in time to your noted bowing and scraping,
our faces all express the naked, rapt
stupidity which more than other arts
yours can evoke, wearing our masks away
till pride relaxes and hypocrisy
forgets his knowing smile—we might be cows
rather than cousins of Mme. Verdurin.

The vacuous expressions of lovers, mourners,
children and pregnant women, people asleep,
racial and strange and sullenly at ease
as African faces or roughly featured stones
with looks eroded in the rain of time,
those were the faces waiting in our faces
for your divisions to divide us from
ourselves till we lost the burden in the ground.

Lascivious dances, melancholy songs,
whose right articulation strikes us dumb,
these shake us in a core that wit forgets
and self wants to deny, in tomb-town where
the dancing-steps are beating in the streets,
where maskers carry away both flower crown
and flowerless torch; from such unsounded chambers,
heartbeaten, how have the dead comforted us!

Some shapes cannot be seen in a glass,
those are the ones the heart breaks at.
They will never become valentines
or crucifixes, never. Night clouds
go on insanely as themselves
though metaphors would be prettier;
and when I see them massed at the edge
of the globe, neither weasel nor whale,
as though this world were, after all,
non-representational, I know
a truth that cannot be told, although
I try to tell you, "We are alone,
we know nothing, nothing, we shall die
frightened in our freedom, the one
who survives will change his name
to evade the vengeance for love. . . ."
Meanwhile the clouds go on clowning
over our heads in the floodlight of
a moon who is known to be Artemis
and Cynthia but sails away anyhow
beyond the serious poets with their
crazy ladies and cloudy histories,
their heroes in whose idiot dreams
the buzzard circles like a clock.

# The Scales of the Eyes

*a poem in the form of a text and variations*

### I

To fleece the Fleece from golden sheep,
Or prey, or get—is it not lewd
That we be eaten by our food
And slept by sleepers in our sleep?

### II

Sleep in the zero, sleep in the spore
Beyond the fires of Orion's hair,
Hard by the spiral burning dust;
Time being Always going west,
Let it be your dream.

Sleep sound in the spaceless lost
Curve running a blind coast;
Number and name, stretch the line
Out on the liquid of the brain,
Begin a falling dream.

The eye will flower in your night
A monstrous bulb, the broth of light
Stew in the marshes of a star;
Death is the wages of what you are,
Life is your long dream.

### III

Around the city where I live
Dead men in their stone towns
Wait out the weather lying down,
And spread widely underground
The salt vines of blood.

Trains run a roaming sound
Under the wired shine of sun and rain.
Black sticks stand up in the sky
Where the wild rails cross and sprawl
Fast and still.

Out there beyond the island
The sea pounds a free way through,
Her wide tides spread on the sand
Stick and brine and rolling stone
The long weather long.

IV

Beneath my foot the secret beast
Whispers, and its stone sinews
Tremble with strength. In the dark earth
Iron winds its tangled nerves,
And the worm eats of the rock
There by the old waters.

Down in dark the rich comb
Gathers wrath out of the light,
The dead ploughed down in their graves
Record the canceled seed its doom.
City, white lion among waters,
Who settest thy claw upon the time,

Measure the tape, wind the clock,
Keep track of weather, watch water
And the work of trains. The bees hum
The honeyed doom of time and time
Again, and riddle this underground
How sweetness comes from the great strength.

V

*(a can of Dutch Cleanser)*

The blind maid shaking a stick,
Chasing dirt endlessly around
A yellow wall, was the very she
To violate my oldest nights;
I frighten of her still.

Her faceless bonnet flaps in wind
I cannot feel, she rages on,
The mad Margery of my sleep;
The socks wrinkle about her shoes
As she drats a maiden dream.

So shines her bleached virginity
On underground conveniences
That roar at once in porcelain hunger;
Her anger leaves me without stain
And white grits in the tub.

VI

The angry voice has sought me out,
Loud-speakers shout among the trees.
What use to hide? He made it all,
Already old when I began.

He held it all upon his knee
And spoke it soft in a big voice
Not so much loud as everywhere,
And all things had to answer him.

This world is not my oyster, nor
No slow socratic pearl grows here.
But the blind valves are closing
On only one grain of sand.

## VII

The low sky was mute and white
And the sun a white hole in the sky
That morning when it came on to snow;
The hushed flakes fell all day.

The hills were hidden in a white air
And every bearing went away,
Landmarks being but white and white
For anyone going anywhere.

All lines were lost, a noon bell
I heard sunk in a sullen pool
Miles off. And yet this patient snow,
When later I walked out in it,

Had lodged itself in tips of grass
And made its mantle bridging so
It lay upon the air and not the earth
So light it hardly bent a blade.

## VIII

From the road looking to the hill I saw
One hollow house hunched in the shoulder.
Windows blinded in a level sun
Stared with not random malice,
Though I had not been in that place.

But I have seen, at the white shore,
The crab eaten in the house of self
And the torn dog shark gutted in sand;
The whole sky goes white with silence
And bears on a few brazen flies.

As though the ground sighed under the foot
And the heart refused its blood; there is
No place I do not taste again
When I choke back the deeper sleep
Beneath the mined world I walk.

## IX

Striding and turning, the caged sea
Knocks at the stone and falls away,
Will not rest night or day
Pacing to be free.

The spiral shell, held at the ear,
Hums the ocean or the blood
A distant cry, misunderstood
Of the mind in the coiled air.

## X

Roads lead to the sea, and then?
The signs drown in the blowing sand,
The breathing and smoothing tide.
It has been a long journey so far.
Gull, where do I go now?

No matter what girls have been laid
In this sand, or far-wandering birds
Died here, I think I will not know
What no galling road has told,
Why to be here or how.

Question the crab, the wasted moon,
The spume blown of the smashed wave,
Ask Polaris about the fish.
No good. I could go home, but there is
No way to go but back.


XI

Plunged the tunnel with the wet wall
Through, sounding with sea space
And the shaken earth, I fell below
The shark diving and the wry worm.
Blindly I nudged a gasping sky.

Against drowning to be born in a caul
Is well. But all free engines
Race to burn themselves out, tear up
The earth and the air and choke on a mouth
Of dirt, throwing their oil.

In long halls of hospital, the white
Eye peeled beneath the pool of light;
Then the blinded, masked and stifled sky
Screamed silver when it grated bone
Beaching a stained keel.

But at last the moon swung dark and away
And waters withered to a salt.
Parched and shaken on a weaned world
I was in wonder burning cold
And in darkness did rest.

## XII

In the water cave, below the root,
The blind fish knew my veins.
I heard ticking the water drop,
The sighing where the wind fell,
When the bat laddered the black air.

Chalk and bone and salt and stone.
Let mother water begin me again,
For I am blackened with burning, gone
From the vain fire of the air,
The one salamander weather.

Slow cold salt, weeds washed
Under crumbling rock ledges
In the water cave below the root,
Quiet the crystal in the dark,
Let the blind way shine out.

## XIII

Gone the armies on the white roads,
The priests blessing and denouncing,
Gone the aircraft speaking power
Through the ruined and echoing air;
And life and death are here.

The quiet pool, if you will listen,
Hisses with your blood, winds
Together vine and vein and thorn,
The thin twisted threads red
With the rust of breath.

Now is the hour in the wild garden
Grown blessed. Tears blinding the eyes,
The martyr's wound and the hurt heart
Seal and are dumb, the ram waits
In the thicket of nerves.

## XIV

In the last hour of the dream
The eye turned upon itself
And stood at bay, peering among
The salt fibers of its blood.

String of the cradle and the kite,
Vine twisted against the bone,
Salt tears washing the sinews,
The spider strangled in her web.

I stood in the last wilderness
Watching the grass at the sea's edge
Bend as to the breathing touch
Of a blind slither at the stalk.

String of the navel and the net,
Vein threading the still pool,
Dumb fingers in the wet sand
Where the heart bled its secret food.

Salt of the flesh, I knew the world
For the white veil over the eye,
The eye for the caged water of light;
The beast asleep in the bleeding snare.


XV

And the rabbis have said the last word
And the iron gates they have slammed shut
Closing my body from the world.
Around me all Long Island lies
Smouldering and still.

Cold winter, the roller coasters
Stand in the swamps by the sea, and bend
The lizards of their bones alone,
August of lust and the hot dog
Frozen in their fat.

But the sea goes her own way,
Around and down her barren green
Sliding and sucking the cold flesh
Of the wrinkled world, with no bone
To such mother-makings.

I have sept through the wide seine.
From Coney Island to Phlegethon
Is no great way by ferris wheel,
And we informal liquors may
Easily despise your bones.

## XVI

Snow on the beaches, briny ice,
Grass white and cracking with the cold.
The light is from the ocean moon
Hanging in the dead height.

Gull rises in the snowy marsh
A shale of light flaked from a star,
The white hair of the breaking wave
Splashes the night sky.

Down at the root, in the warm dream,
The lily bows among the ruins.
Kingdoms rise and are blown down
While the summer fly hums.

## XVII

When black water breaks the ice
The moon is milk and chalk of tooth.
The star is bleeding in the still pool
And the horny skin is left behind
When journey must be new-begun.

Teiresias watching in the wood
A wheel of snakes, gave his sight
To know the coupled work of time,
How pale woman and fiery man
Married their disguise away.

Then all was the self, but self was none;
Knowing itself in the fiery dark
The blind pool of the eye became
The sailing of the moon and sun
Through brightness melted into sky.


XVIII

Of leaf and branch and rain and light,
The spider's web glistered with wet,
The robin's breast washed red in sun
After the rapid storm goes on;

Of long light level on the lake
And white on the side of lonely houses,
The thunder going toward the hill,
The last lightning cracking the sky;

New happiness of everything!
The blind worm lifts up his head
And the sparrow shakes a wet wing
In the home of little while.

# The Winter Lightning

*for Paul*

Over the snow at night,
And while the snow still fell,
A sky torn to the bone
Shattered the ghostly world with light;
As though this were the moon's hell,
A world hard as a stone,
  Cold, and blue-white.

As if the storming sea
Should sunder to its floor,
And all things hidden there
Gleam in the moment silently,
So does the meadow at the door
To split and sudden air
  Show stone and tree.

From the drowned world of dark
The sleeping innocence
Surrenders all its seeming;
Under the high, charged carbon arc
Light of the world, a guilty sense
Stiffens the secret dreaming
  Animal park.

So in the camera's glare
The fortunate and famed,
For all their crooked smiles,
Reveal through their regarded stare
How all that's publicly acclaimed
One brutal flash reviles
  For cold despair.

So is the murderer caught
When his lost victim rises
Glaring through dream and light
With icy eyes. That which was thought
In secret, and after wore disguises,
Silts up the drowning sight
   Mind inwrought.

So may the poem dispart
The mirror from the light
Where none can see a seam;
The poet, from his wintry heart
And in the lightning second's sight,
Illuminate this dream
   With a cold art.

# I Only Am Escaped Alone To Tell Thee

I tell you that I see her still
At the dark entrance of the hall.
One gas lamp burning near her shoulder
Shone also from her other side
Where hung the long inaccurate glass
Whose pictures were as troubled water.
An immense shadow had its hand
Between us on the floor, and seemed
To hump the knuckles nervously,
A giant crab readying to walk,
Or a blanket moving in its sleep.

You will remember, with a smile
Instructed by movies to reminisce,
How strict her corsets must have been,
How the huge arrangements of her hair
Would certainly betray the least
Impassionate displacement there.
It was no rig for dallying,
And maybe only marriage could
Derange that queenly scaffolding—
As when a great ship, coming home,
Coasts in the harbor, dropping sail
And loosing all the tackle that had laced
Her in the long lanes  . . .
                              I know
We need not draw this figure out
But all that whalebone came from whales
And all the whales lived in the sea,
In calm beneath the troubled glass,
Until the needle drew their blood.

I see her standing in the hall,
Where the mirror's lashed to blood and foam,
And the black flukes of agony
Beat at the air till the light blows out.

# *Writing*

The cursive crawl, the squared-off characters,
these by themselves delight, even without
a meaning, in a foreign language, in
Chinese, for instance, or when skaters curve
all day across the lake, scoring their white
records in ice. Being intelligible,
these winding ways with their audacities
and delicate hesitations, they become
miraculous, so intimately, out there
at the pen's point or brush's tip, do world
and spirit wed. The small bones of the wrist
balance against great skeletons of stars
exactly; the blind bat surveys his way
by echo alone. Still, the point of style
is character. The universe induces
a different tremor in every hand, from the
check-forger's to that of the Emperor
Hui Tsung, who called his own calligraphy
the 'Slender Gold.' A nervous man
writes nervously of a nervous world, and so on.

Miraculous. It is as though the world
were a great writing. Having said so much,
let us allow there is more to the world
than writing; continental faults are not
bare convoluted fissures in the brain.
Not only must the skaters soon go home;
also the hard inscription of their skates
is scored across the open water, which long
remembers nothing, neither wind nor wake.

      —Ah, green Elysia,
Scuttled at last into the western sea,
Thou crownèd, fragile sea-nymph, slender bodied,
Thy lobes and processes have trancèd me,
My lust beguns to rule.
               —False Wentletrap!
Avaunt. My maiden mantle may not blush
For thee or thine, all towering as thou art
And turreted. For thee do I disdain
As doth the warty Venus of the shore
The prickly cockle's Tarquin-like approach.
Sea-lemon, with thy tricksy tentacles
And feather-gills, thou granulated thing,
I deprecate on thee.
           —Alas! I pale,
And all my whorls 'gin waver. Wrinkle me,
Or else I perish.
         —Horny, let thy drawn
Operculum defend thee now.
             —Elysia,
Upon thy cruel tentacles I die.

—And now I am alone.

# *To Lu Chi*

(*author of the Wen Fu, or Prose Poem on the Art of Letters,*
A.D. 302)

Old sir, I think of you in this tardy spring,
Think of you for, maybe, no better reason
Than that the apple branches in the orchard
Bear snow, not blossoms, and that this somehow
Seems oddly Chinese. I too, when I walk
Around the orchard, pretending to be a poet
Walking around the orchard, feel Chinese,
A silken figure on a silken screen
Who tries out with his eye the apple branches,
The last year's shriveled apples capped with snow,
The hungry birds. And then I think of you.

Through many centuries of dust, to which
We both belong, your quiet voice is clear
About the difficulties and delights
Of writing well, which are, it seems, always
The same and generally unfashionable.
In all the many times I have read your poem,
Or treatise, where the art of letters turns
To the inspection of itself—the theme
(I take your phrase) of how to hold the axe
To make its handle,—your words have not failed
To move me with their justice and their strength,
Their manner gentle as their substance is
Fastidious and severe. You frighten me
When you describe the dangers of our course,
And then you bring, by precept and example,
Assurance that a reach of mastery,
Some still, reed-hidden and reflective stream
Where the heron fishes in his own image,

Always exists. I have a sight of you,
Your robes tucked in your belt, standing
Fishing that stream, where it is always dawn
With a mist beginning to be burned away
By the lonely sun. And soon you will turn back
To breakfast and the waking of the world
Where the contending war lords and the lords
Of money pay to form the public taste
For their derivative sonorities;
But yet that pure and hidden reach remains.

Lu Chi, it's said the world has changed, and that
Is doubtless something which is always said
(Though now to justify, and not in scorn)—
Yet I should think that on our common theme
That sort of change has never mattered much.
In letters as in many other trades
The active man and the contemplative
May both engage, and both in different ways
Succeed. The alphabet, the gift of god
Or of the gods (and modern as we are,
We have no better theory yet), was not
Devised to one use only, but to all
The work that human wit could find for it;
Is honorably employed in government
And all techniques; without it, nothing. Yet
The active man, because he is active,
Expropriates as if by natural right
The common ground to his singular use,
And spits on everything he cannot use;

Not knowing, or not caring, that to use
Means also to use up. So I have read,
In works by sages of the active side,
And heard them say, that poetry is dead.
This ancient paragon and type of arts,
They say, was magic when the world began,
And when the old magacians died in scorn
Among the ruins of unsuccessful spells,
Their childish children, living in the dawn
Of intellect and conscience, said those spells
(Which could not move a mountain or a mouse
In a real world) for courage and consolation,
Making those holy places in their hearts
Not masonry nor magic made elsewhere.
But now, in the objective, brazen light
Shed by the sciences, they say, the arts,
And poetry first, considered as their trunk,
The nearest to the root, and bearing branches
Aloft with flower and fruit, and spreading seed
To all societies, must wither away
By supersession in nature and all hearts.
So in our day wisdom cries out in the streets
And some men regard her. And in your day,
Lu Chi? We know these theories, which are not new,
And know the sort of man these theories
Produce, intelligent and serviceable
So long as he can see his language as
Coin of the realm, backed up by church and state,
Each word referring to a thing, each thing
Nicely denominated by a word—

A good mind at its best, a trifle dry. . . .
But in bad times, when the word of command
Fails to command, and when the word for bread
Dries and grows mouldy, he is, of all men,
The likeliest to panic as he sits
In his bomb shelter and commissions war songs
From active poets with aggressive views.
Nor on the day when all civilization
Quite visibly and audibly collapses,
When Paris burns as merrily as Sodom,
When London looks like Hell, or Hiroshima,
Not even then, will this man of his own
Free choice consult those who consult the source—
Who by then, in any case, can do nothing.
Meanwhile, in riches, insolence and honor
Pride is twisting his tongue. What an old joke!
These things, Lu Chi, cannot have changed so much.

What then? Nothing but this, old sir: *continue*.
And to the active man, if he should ask
(If he should bother asking) Why? say nothing.
And to the thinker, if he should ask us once
Instead of telling us, again say nothing.
But look into the clear and mirroring stream
Where images remain although the water
Passes away. Neither action nor thought,
Only the concentration of our speech
In fineness and in strength (your axe again),
Till it can carry, in those other minds,
A nobler action and a purer thought.

So much I gather from your poem: *continue*.
And now the sun shines on the apple trees,
The melting snow glitters with a great wealth,
The waxwings, drunk on last year's rotten apples,
Move through the branches, uttering pretty cries,
While portly grosbeaks, because they do not drink
That applejack, chatter with indignation.
How fine the Chinese day! delicate, jeweled,
Exactly spaced, peaceably tense with life.
I shall pretend to be a poet all
This afternoon, a Chinese poet, and
My marvelous words must bring the springtime in
And the great tree of speech to flower
Between the two realms of heaven and earth. So now
Goodbye, Lu Chi, and thank you for your poem.

## Zalmoxis

The way spring comes this time, with a soft
Suddenness: after the robin-snow a rain,
After the rain the sun in a ragged cloud
Making a mild mist on the cold meadows,
On stone walls veined with ice, on blind windows
Burnt red beneath the southward slate of houses.

From the pale, yellow and peeled branches of willow
And alder the globes of water grow and fall
In ripenings of light; and a crystal thread,
Enlaced with the needles of the pine, silvers
The earliest sketches of the spider, softens
Coldly to life the leaves of pupal sleep.

Warm in the house, at the bright window's edge,
A fly crawls on the dry, leathery spines
Of the sleeping dramatists; the speckled dust,
In the long light's line between the blinds,
Dances until the scholar's ancient eye
Lights between sleep and waking. He leaves his book,

And, rising, he throws open the window wide,
Watches cigar smoke swaying in the room
Till smoke and dream dissolve in air together;
Then stares down the field to the wild hill,
Where on this day the sullen and powerful bear,
Drunken with deathlessness, lurches from sleep.

# Dandelions

These golden heads, these common suns
Only less multitudinous
Than grass itself that gluts
The market of the world with green,
They shine as lovely as they're mean,
Fine as the daughters of the poor
Who go proudly in spangles of brass;
Light-headed, then headless, stalked for a salad.

Inside a week they will be seen
Stricken and old, ghosts in the field
To be picked up at the lightest breath
With brazen tops all shrunken in
And swollen green gone withered white.
You'll say it's nature's price for beauty
That goes cheap; that being light
Is justly what makes girls grow heavy;
And that the wind, bearing their death,
Whispers the second kingdom come
—You'll say, the fool of piety,
By resignations hanging on
Until, still justified, you drop.
But surely the thing is sorrowful,
At evening, when the light goes out
Slowly, to see those ruined spinsters,
All down the field their ghostly hair,
Dry sinners waiting in the valley
For the last word and the next life
And the liberation from the lion's mouth.

## Suburban Prophecy

On Saturday, the power-mowers' whine
Begins the morning. Over this neighborhood
Rises the keening, petulant voice, begin
Green oily teeth to chatter and munch the cud.

Monsters, crawling the carpets of the world,
Still send from underground against your blades
The roots of things battalions green and curled
And tender, that will match your blades with blades
Till the revolted throats shall strangle on
The tickle of their dead, till straws shall break
Crankshafts like camels, and the sun go down
On dinosaurs in swamps. A night attack
Follows, and by the time the Sabbath dawns
All armored beasts are eaten by their lawns.

# The Goose Fish

On the long shore, lit by the moon
To show them properly alone,
Two lovers suddenly embraced
So that their shadows were as one.
The ordinary night was graced
For them by the swift tide of blood
That silently they took at flood,
And for a little time they prized
   Themselves emparadised.

Then, as if shaken by stage-fright
Beneath the hard moon's bony light,
They stood together on the sand
Embarrassed in each other's sight
But still conspiring hand in hand,
Until they saw, there underfoot,
As though the world had found them out,
The goose fish turning up, though dead,
   His hugely grinning head.

There in the china light he lay,
Most ancient and corrupt and grey
They hesitated at his smile,
Wondering what it seemed to say
To lovers who a little while
Before had thought to understand,
By violence upon the sand,
The only way that could be known
   To make a world their own.

It was a wide and moony grin
Together peaceful and obscene;
They knew not what he would express,
So finished a comedian
He might mean failure or success,
But took it for an emblem of
Their sudden, new and guilty love
To be observed by, when they kissed,
    That rigid optimist.

So he became their patriarch,
Dreadfully mild in the half-dark.
His throat that the sand seemed to choke,
His picket teeth, these left their mark
But never did explain the joke
That so amused him, lying there
While the moon went down to disappear
Along the still and tilted track
    That bears the zodiac.

# Midsummer's Day

*for my son*

A misty heat, now that the spring has gone,
Glitters out on this hillside and the meadow,
Over the bend where the slow river turns
To be lost among willows. Hardly a shadow
But the high sun seems to see through, who burns
As from within, till the green world goes brown
Under the skin, and the heights of summer lie
Parched with life at the lid of the mind's eye.

This ruinous garden an old woman made
And fertilized with tea leaves and coffee grounds,
Is wild grass mostly, climbed up to the thigh;
The multitude of dandelion surrounds
Enclaves of iris and opening peony;
While at the wall, the handle of a spade
Is toughly fastened in a climbing vine
That's crawled among blue flowers, serpentine.

I have looked out and seen the summer grow
Day after day between the cracked flags
Of the terrace where no one wishes to sit,
And thought of fortune and family, the fine rags
Brutal desire, poor patience, or a nice wit
Had made to be stitched together in a show
For everyone to marvel at, a pride
That must have been already withered inside.

This place belonged to farming people once—
Maybe a pity that it doesn't now;
For any mind, even on the summer's side,
Will let it go, cabbage chicken and cow,
From piety of sorts, or for the ride
Downhill on history, seeing that fate runs
Wild as the summer—Babylon and Rome,
As ruin remains, brought in a sense home.

Ruin remains, and nature pays no mind.
This mind, that flesh is and will go like grass
In the brief stubble burnt at harvest or
In the sun's long stare, sees as though sealed in glass
The high and silent wave over the floor
Of summer come, casting up seed and rind;
And, held upon this hill, among the trees
Hears the loud forage of the honey bees.

# The Town Dump

*"The art of our necessities is strange,*
*That can make vile things precious."*

A mile out in the marshes, under a sky
Which seems to be always going away
In a hurry, on that Venetian land threaded
With hidden canals, you will find the city
Which seconds ours (so cemeteries, too,
Reflect a town from hillsides out of town),
Where Being most Becomingly ends up
Becoming some more. From cardboard tenements,
Windowed with cellophane, or simply tenting
In paper bags, the angry mackerel eyes
Glare at you out of stove-in, sunken heads
Far from the sea; the lobster, also, lifts
An empty claw in his most minatory
Of gestures; oyster, crab, and mussel shells
Lie here in heaps, savage as money hurled
Away at the gate of hell. If you want results,
These are results.
                    Objects of value or virtue,
However, are also to be picked up here,
Though rarely, lying with bones and rotten meat,
Eggshells and mouldy bread, banana peels
No one will skid on, apple cores that caused
Neither the fall of man nor a theory
Of gravitation. People do throw out
The family pearls by accident, sometimes,
Not often; I've known dealers in antiques
To prowl this place by night, with flashlights, on
The off-chance of somebody's having left
Derelict chairs which will turn out to be
By Hepplewhite, a perfect set of six
Going to show, I guess, that in any sty
Someone's heaven may open and shower down

Riches responsive to the right dream; though
It is a small chance, certainly, that sends
The ghostly dealer, heavy with fly-netting
Over his head, across these hills in darkness,
Stumbling in cut-glass goblets, lacquered cups,
And other products of his dreamy midden
Penciled with light and guarded by the flies.

For there are flies, of course. A dynamo
Composed, by thousands, of our ancient black
Retainers, hums here day and night, steady
As someone telling beads, the hum becoming
A high whine at any disturbance; then,
Settled again, they shine under the sun
Like oil-drops, or are invisible as night,
By night.
        All this continually smoulders,
Crackles, and smokes with mostly invisible fires
Which, working deep, rarely flash out and flare,
And never finish. Nothing finishes;
The flies, feeling the heat, keep on the move.

Among the flies, the purefying fires,
The hunters by night, acquainted with the art
Of our necessities, and the new deposits
That each day wastes with treasure, you may say
There should be ratios. You may sum up
The results, if you want results. But I will add
That wild birds, drawn to the carrion and flies,
Assemble in some numbers here, their wings
Shining with light, their flight enviably free,
Their music marvelous, though sad, and strange.

## *Shells*

You pick one up along the shore.
It is empty and light and dry,
And leaves a powdery chalk on your hands.

The life that made it is gone out.
That is what is meant when people say,
"A hollow shell," "a shell of his former self,"

Failing to take into account
The vital waste in composition
With the beauty of the ruined remainder

Which is no use to anyone,
Of course, unless as decoration:
A Souvenir of Sunset Beach, etc.

Its form is only cryptically
Instructive, if at all: it winds
Like generality, from nothing to nothing

By means of nothing but itself.
It is a stairway going nowhere,
Our precious emblem of the steep ascent,

Perhaps, beginning at a point
And opening to infinity,
Or the other way, if you want it the other way.

Inside it, also, there is nothing
Except the obedient sound of waters
Beat by your Mediterranean, classic heart

In bloody tides as long as breath,
Bringing by turns the ebb and flood
Upon the ruining house of histories,

Whose whitening stones, in Africa,
Bake dry and blow away, in Athens,
In Rome, abstract and instructive as chalk

When children scrawl the blackboard full
Of wild spirals every which way,
To be erased with chalk dust, then with water.

# A Day on the Big Branch

Still half drunk, after a night at cards,
with the grey dawn taking us unaware
among our guilty kings and queens, we drove
far North in the morning, winners, losers,
to a stream in the high hills, to climb up to a place
one of us knew, with some vague view
of cutting losses or consolidating gains
by the old standard appeal to the wilderness,
the desert, the empty places of our exile,
bringing only the biblical bread and cheese
and cigarettes got from a grocer's on the way,
expecting to drink only the clear cold water
among the stones, and remember, or forget.
Though no one said anything about atonement,
there was still some purgatorial idea
in all those aching heads and ageing hearts
as we climbed the giant stair of the stream,
reaching the place around noon.

It was as promised, a wonder, with granite walls
enclosing ledges, long and flat, of limestone,
or, rolling, of lava; within the ledges
the water, fast and still, pouring its yellow light
and green, over the tilted slabs of the floor,
blackened at shady corners, falling in a foam
of crystal to a calm where the waterlight
dappled the ledges as they leaned
against the sun; big blue dragonflies hovered
and darted and dipped a wing, hovered again
against the low wind moving over the stream,
and shook the flakes of light from their clear wings.
This surely was it, was what we had come for,

was nature, though it looked like art with its
grey fortress walls and laminated benches
as in the waiting room of some petrified station.
But we believed; and what it was we believed
made of the place a paradise
for ruined poker players, win or lose,
who stripped naked and bathed and dried out on the rocks
like gasping trout (the water they drank
making them drunk again), lit cigarettes and lay back
waiting for nature to say the last word
—as though the stones were Memnon stones,
which, caught in a certain light, would sing.

The silence (and even the noise of the waters
was silence) grew pregnant; that is the phrase,
grew pregnant; but nothing else did.
The mountain brought forth not a mouse, and the rocks,
unlike the ones you would expect to find
on the slopes of Purgatory or near Helicon,
mollified by muses and with a little give to 'em,
were modern American rocks, and hard as rocks.
Our easy bones groaned, our flesh baked
on one side and shuddered on the other; and each man
thought bitterly about primitive simplicity
and decadence, and how he had been ruined
by civilization and forced by circumstances
to drink and smoke and sit up all night
inspecting those perfectly arbitrary cards
until he was broken-winded as a trout on a rock
and had no use for the doctrines of Jean Jacques
Rousseau, and could no longer afford
a savagery whether noble or not; some
would never batter that battered copy of Walden
again.

But all the same,
the water, the sunlight, and the wind
did something; even the dragonflies
did something to the minds full of telephone
numbers and flushes, to the flesh
sweating bourbon on one side and freezing on the other.
And the rocks, the old and tumbling boulders
which formed the giant stair of the stream,
induced (again) some purgatorial ideas
concerning humility, concerning patience
and enduring what had to be endured,
winning and losing and breaking even;
ideas of weathering in whatever weather,
being eroded, or broken, or ground down into pebbles
by the stream's necessitous and grave currents.
But to these ideas did any purgatory
respond? Only this one: that in a world
where even the Memnon stones were carved in soap
one might at any rate wash with the soap.

After a time we talked about the War,
about what we had done in the War, and how near
some of us had been to being drowned, and burned,
and shot, and how many people we knew
who had been drowned, or burned, or shot;
and would it have been better to have died
in the War, the peaceful old War, where we were young?
But the mineral peace, or paralysis, of those
great stones, the moving stillness of the waters,
entered our speech; the ribs and blood
of the earth, from which all fables grow,
established poetry and truth in us,

so that at last one said, "I shall play cards
until the day I die," and another said,
"in bourbon whisky are all the vitamins
and minerals needed to sustain man's life,"
and still another, "I shall live on smoke
until my spirit has been cured of flesh."

Climbing downstream again, on the way home
to the lives we had left empty for a day,
we noticed, as not before, how of three bridges
not one had held the stream, which in its floods
had twisted the girders, splintered the boards, hurled
boulder on boulder, and had broken into rubble,
smashed practically back to nature,
the massive masonry of span after span
with its indifferent rage; this was a sight
that sobered us considerably, and kept us quiet
both during the long drive home and after,
till it was time to deal the cards.

# Deep Woods

Such places are too still for history,
Which slows, shudders, and shifts as the trucks do,
In hearing-distance, on the highway hill,
And staggers onward elsewhere with its load
Of statues, candelabra, buttons, gold;
But here the heart, racing strangely as though
Ready to stop, reaches a kind of rest;
The mind uneasily rests, as if a beast,
Being hunted down, made tiredness and terror
Its camouflage and fell asleep, and dreamed,
At the terrible, smooth pace of the running dogs,
A dream of being lost, covered with leaves
And hidden in a death like any sleep
So deep the bitter world must let it be
And go bay elsewhere after better game.
Even the restless eye, racing upon
Reticulated branch and vine which go
Nowhere, at last returns upon itself
And comes into a flickering kind of rest,
Being lost in the insanity of line.

Line, leaf, and light; darkness invades our day;
No meaning in it, but indifference
Which does not flatter with profundity.
Nor is it drama. Even the giant oak,
Stricken a hundred years or yesterday,
Has not found room to fall as heroes should
But crookedly leans on an awkward-squad of birch,
The tragic image and the mighty crash
Indefinitely delayed in favor of

Fresh weaving of vines, rooting of outer branches,
Beginning again, in spaces still more cramped,
A wandering calligraphy which seems
Enthralled to a magic constantly misspelled.

It is the same, they say, everywhere.
But that's not so. These here are the deep woods
Of now, New England, this October, when
Dry gold has little left to change, and half
The leaves are gone to ground, and half of those
Rained into the leaf-mold which tenses in
The fastenings of frost; where the white branches
Of birch are dry bones airborne in assaults
Which haven't worked yet. This unlegended land
Is no Black Forest where the wizard lived
Under a bent chimney and a thatch of straw;
Nor the hot swamp theatrical with snakes
And tigers; nor the Chinese forest on
The mountainside, with bridge, pagoda, fog,
Three poets in the foreground, drinking tea
(there is no tea, and not so many as three)—
But this land, this, unmitigated by myth
And whose common splendors are comparable only to
Themselves; this leaf, line, light, are scrawled alone
In solar definitions on a lump
Of hill like nothing known since Nature was
Invented by Watteau or Fragonard
In the Old Kingdom or the time of Set
Or before the Flood of Yao (or someone else
Of the same name) in the Fourth, or Disney, Dimension.

And this is yours to work; plant it to salt
Or men in armor who destroy each other,
Sprinkle with dragon's blood early in spring
And see what happens, epic or pastoral:
A sword in every stone, small minotaurs
Looking for thread, and unicorns for girls,
And Glastonbury thorns to make December
Bleed for the Saviour; the nightingale of Sarras
Enchants the traveler here three hundred years
And a day which seem but as a single day.
More probably nothing will happen. This
Place is too old for history to know
Beans about; these trees were here, are here,
Before King Hannibal had elephants
Or Frederick grew his red beard through the table
Or Mordecai hung Haman at the gate.
The other Ahasuerus has not spat
Nor walked nor cobbled any shoe, nor Joseph
So much as dreamed that he will found the Corn
Exchange Bank in the baked country of Egypt.
Not even those burnt beauties are hawked out,
By the angry Beginner, on Chaos floor
Where they build Pandemonium the Palace
Back in the high old times. Most probably
Nothing will happen. Even the Fall of Man
Is waiting, here, for someone to grow apples;
And the snake, speckled as sunlight on the rock
In the deep woods, still sleeps with a whole head
And has not begun to grow a manly smile.

# Sunday at the End of Summer

Last night the cold wind and the rain blew
Hard from the west, all night, until the creek
Flooded, tearing the end of a wooden bridge
Down to hang, trembling, in the violent water.

This morning, with the weather still in rage,
I watched workmen already at repairs.
Some hundred of us came around to watch,
With collars turned against the rain and wind.

Down the wild water, where men stood to the knees,
We saw come flooding hollyhock and vine,
Sunflowers tall and broken, thorny bramble
And pale lilies cracked along the stalk.

Ours was the Sunday's perfect idleness
To watch those others working; who fought, swore,
Being threshed at hip and thigh, against that trash
Of pale wild flowers and their drifting legs.

## Brainstorm

The house was shaken by a rising wind
That rattled window and door. He sat alone
In an upstairs room and heard these things: a blind
Ran up with a bang, a door slammed, a groan
Came from some hidden joist, a leaky tap,
At any silence of the wind  walked like
A blind man through the house. Timber and sap
Revolt, he thought, from washer, baulk and spike.
Bent to his book, continued unafraid
Until the crows came down from their loud flight
To walk along the rooftree overhead.
Their horny feet, so near but out of sight,
Scratched on the slate; when they were blown away
He heard their wings beat till they came again,
While the wind rose, and the house seemed to sway,
And window panes began to blind with rain.
The house was talking, not to him, he thought,
But to the crows; the crows were talking back
In their black voices. The secret might be out:
Houses are only trees stretched on the rack.
And once the crows knew, all nature would know.
Fur, leaf and feather would invade the form,
Nail rust with rain and shingle warp with snow,
Vine tear the wall, till any straw-borne storm
Could rip both roof and rooftree off and show
Naked to nature what they had kept warm.

He came to feel the crows walk on his head
As if he were the house, their crooked feet
Scratched, through the hair, his scalp. He might be dead,
It seemed, and all the noises underneath
Be but the cooling of the sinews, veins,
Juices, and sodden sacks suddenly let go;
While in his ruins of wiring, his burst mains,
The rainy wind had been set free to blow
Until the green uprising and mob rule
That ran the world had taken over him,
Split him like seed, and set him in the school
Where any crutch can learn to be a limb.

Inside his head he heard the stormy crows.

# The Sanctuary

Over a ground of slate and light gravel,
Clear water, so shallow that one can see
The numerous springs moving their mouths of sand;
And the dark trout are clearly to be seen,
Swimming this water which is color of air
So that the fish appear suspended nowhere and
In nothing. With a delicate bend and reflex
Of their tails the trout slowly glide
From the shadowy side into the light, so clear,
And back again into the shadows; slow
And so definite, like thought emerging
Into a clear place in the mind, then going back,
Exchanging shape for shade. Now and again
One fish slides into the center of the pool
And hangs between the surface and the slate
For several minutes without moving, like
A silence in a dream; and when I stand
At such a time, observing this, my life
Seems to have been suddenly moved a great
Distance away on every side, as though
The quietest thought of all stood in the pale
Watery light alone, and was no more
My own than the speckled trout I stare upon
All but unseeing. Even at such times
The mind goes on transposing and revising
The elements of its long allegory
In which the anagoge is always death;
And while this vision blurs with empty tears,

I visit, in the cold pool of the skull,
A sanctuary where the slender trout
Feed on my drowned eyes. . . . Until this trout
Pokes through the fabric of the surface to
Snap up a fly. As if a man's own eyes
Raised welts upon the mirror whence they stared,
I find this world again in focus, and
This fish, a shadow dammed in artifice,
Swims to the furthest shadows out of sight
Though not, in time's ruining stream, out of mind.

*Part III*

*Early Poems*

# The Second-Best Bed

Consider now that Troy has burned
—Priam is dead, and Hector dead,
And great Aeneas long since turned
Away seaward with his gods
To find, found or founder, against frightful odds.

And figure to yourselves the clown
Who comes with educated word
To illustrate in mask and gown
King Priam's most illustrious son
And figure forth his figure with many another one

Of that most ceremented time
In times have been or are to be
Inhearsed in military rime;
And will recite of royal fates
Until, infamonized among those potentates

By a messenger from nearer home,
His comedy is compromised
And he must leave both Greece and Rome
Abuilding but not half begun,
To play the honest Troyan to a girl far gone.

The wench lived on, if the son died—
All Denmark wounded in one bed
Cried vengeance on the lusty bride,
Who could not care that there would follow,
After the words of Mercury, songs of Apollo.

# The Brief Journey West

By the dry road the fathers cough and spit,
This is their room. They are the ones who hung
That bloody sun upon the southern wall
And crushed the armored beetle to the floor.

The fathers' skin is seamed and dry, the map
Of that wild region where they drained the swamp
And set provision out that they might sit,
Of history the cracked precipitate,

Until the glass be shattered and the sun
Descend to burn the prosperous flesh away
Of the filthy world, so vilely fathered on
The fathers, such black cinders, sitting there.

Old pioneers, what lecheries remain?
When schoolgirls pass, what whispers of their skirts,
Cold gleams of flesh, solicit in your veined
And gemlike eyes the custom of desire?

None now. Their eyes are sunk in ancient flesh,
And the sarcastic triumph of the mind
They now enjoy, letting their lust alone
Who may have kin but have no longer kind.

Neither tomorrow's monstrous tumor nor
The reformation of the past they wish,
Who hold in silent colloquy the world
A shrivelled apple in the hand of God.

They hang at night their somber flags aloft,
And through the amorous dark pursue their theme
Of common images, that sleep may show
Them done with all disasters but the one.

# *Carol*

Now is the world withdrawn all
*In silence and night*
To beweeping Adam's fall
That this biography began
Of vile man.

Now the serpent smiles on sin
*In silence and night*
And sees the tumor swell within—
The heavy fruit that was the heart
Beat apart.

The spider's spittle weaves the shroud
*In silence and night*
Wide enough for all the proud;
Gapes the grave in pompous black
At our back.

Christ the King is born again
*In silence and night*
Bringing mercy to all men
Whose separate pride full is beguiled
By this child.

From Eden's Tree the Cross is made
*In silence and night*
Where Adam's bondman now is nailed
While the wild multitude
Cries for blood.

The great grave stone is rolled away
*In silence and night*
And He arose on the third day
That Adam might, free of the chains,
Choose his pains

And follow Him upon the Cross
*In silence and night*
And disdain all worldly loss
And to the compassionate King
Pray and sing.

Therefore do we cross this hour
*In silence and night*
Our grief and joy, weakness and power,
Whereto Christ's glory and His pain
Both constrain.

For there was born at Bethlehem
*In silence and night*
The world's and heaven's single stem
That to both kingdoms we might then
Say Amen.

# Fables of the Moscow Subway

The earthly doctor fiddled with his beard,
Considered the spiders Svidrigailov saw
Climbing the bath-house of eternity.
Man lives, he said, only by parricide.

Madame la Mothe had lovers one two three
Moonlit among the Dresden figurines.
And her brocaded dress was thumbed aside
Silently, and her heavy hair caressed.

The displaced persons wandered all this while
Through everglades where the loud-shrieking worm
Struggled in fragile webs; or came beyond
The tragic scene, to temples which were tombs.

The doctor, in an illustrated tome,
Saw mitred bishops creeping from a cave.
In gowns heavy with gold they went haughtily,
He thought, between the knees of Babylon.

Madame la Mothe, after the last man left,
Lifted Venetian blinds upon the town.
The lights were necklaces, and at her feet,
She thought, the world lay flat as a five-pound note.

And when she had coiled up her hair in nets
And nakedly had sunk into pale sleep,
She was as ocean, alone and deep and mute
(The moon being lost now outside the clouds).

But the doctor, with smoldering cigar,
Waked, and went patiently among the dead;
Inquired how their parents were, and when
They last had wet the bed or dreamed of God.

He read in the *Timaeus* once again
That the good old days were gone beneath the sea.
He seemed to understand, coughed once, and slept.
And then it was revealed to him in dream:

*That Martin Luther shrieked aloud, Thou Pope!*
*And fled to England, and created the Boy Scouts,*
*Who were encamped above Lake Titicaca*
*And might invade the Rhineland if they wished.*

# Redeployment

They say the war is over. But water still
Comes bloody from the taps, and my pet cat
In his disorder vomits worms which crawl
Swiftly away. Maybe they leave the house.
These worms are white, and flecked with the cat's blood.

The war may be over. I know a man
Who keeps a pleasant souvenir, he keeps
A soldier's dead blue eyeballs that he found
Somewhere—hard as chalk, and blue as slate.
He clicks them in his pocket while he talks.

And now there are cockroaches in the house,
They get slightly drunk on DDT,
Are fast, hard, shifty—can be drowned but not
Without you hold them under quite some time.
People say the Mexican kind can fly.

The end of the war. I took it quietly
Enough. I tried to wash the dirt out of
My hair and from under my fingernails,
I dressed in clean white clothes and went to bed.
I heard the dust falling between the walls.

After Margrave died, nothing
Seemed worth while. I said as much
To Brumbach, who replied:
"The oscillations of fashion
Do not amuse me. There have been
Great men before, there will be
Other great men. Only man
Is important, man is ultimate."
I can still see him sitting there,
Sipping level by level his
Pousse-café. He was a fat man.
Fat men are seldom the best
Creative writers.
                    The rest of us
Slowly dispersed, hardly
ever saw each other again,
And did not correspond, for
There was little enough to say.
Only Impli and I
Hung on, feeling as we did
That the last word had not
Finally been said. Sometimes
I feel, I might say, cheated.
Life here at Bad Grandstein
Is dull, is dull, what with
The eternal rocks and the river;
And Impli, though one of my
Dearest friends, can never,
I have decided, become great.

# The Stare of the Man from the Provinces

In the metropolis of hooligans
Sweet May reigneth forever. Do you hear
The pale chitter of china wings in windows?
Glass perrokeets preen and silently shrill.

The perfumes of hooligan ladies spill
An old delight upon the ground, their shadows
Couple inconsequentially everywhere.
Peacocks in windows spread up their proud fans.

Indeed the city coruscates with eyes
Both bold and proud, of dames and gentlemen,
That flowerlike upon their haughty stalks
Bulge at the perfect springtime of the streets.

Only at night, between the snowy sheets
Resting infected feet from pleasant walks,
All eyelids close, confine the citizen
Within the echoing caverns of his eyes.

  At night all hooligans in lonely bed
  Must suffer cry of birds they had thought dead.
  And diamond beak, unfashionable nails
  Tear at the eyes until in sleep sight fails.

## The Phoenix

The Phoenix comes of flame and dust
He bundles up his sire in myrrh
A solar and unholy lust
Makes a cradle of his bier

In the City of the Sun
He dies and rises all divine
There is never more than one
Genuine

By incest, murder, suicide
Survives the sacred purple bird
Himself his father, son and bride
And his own Word